VICTORY TO VICTORY

52 WAYS TO STAY HAPPY AND LIVE A VICTORIOUS LIFE

JEROME O. OBODE

Unless otherwise indicated, Scripture quotations are taken from the Holy Bible, King James (Authorized Version). First Published in 1611.

Printed in Great Britain in 2018 by Living Spread Publications

© 2018 by Jerome O. Obode

All rights reserved. No part of this publication may be reproduced, stored in a retrieval system, or transmitted in any form or by any means without written permission from the publisher.

ISBN 978-1-9998798-2-2

London, United Kingdom

www.livingspread.com

Email: livingspread@gmail.com

Dedication

This book is dedicated to all God's precious people around the world who have committed to reading my daily devotional writings. Your feedback, encouragement and support have kept me going over the years. This book is a product of some of the devotionals you told me you have found helpful. I am eternally grateful to you.

CONTENTS

Introduction

1. Look After Yourself --------------------------- 1
2. Leave Your Comfort Zone ------------------ 3
3. See Yourself Accurately--------------------- 5
4. Define Your Own Success------------------ 7
5. Make Reading A Habit--------------------- 9
6. Sow Your Seed------------------------------ 11
7. Let Nothing Stop You---------------------- 13
8. Give Up The Titanic Mentality------------ 15
9. Start Your Day With God------------------ 17
10. Avoid Prejudice Like A Plague------------ 19
11. Keep Growing Spiritually------------------ 21
12. Always Do More Than Is Required------- 23
13. Keep Accelerating-------------------------- 25
14. Take The First Step------------------------ 27
15. Resolve To Win In Difficult Times------- 29
16. Get Rid Of The Little Foxes--------------- 31
17. Never Betray People's Trust-------------- 33
18. Surrender Your Fears To God------------ 35
19. Embrace Change--------------------------- 37
20. Never Fear Your Critics------------------- 39
21. Look After Your Health------------------- 41
22. Reject The Victim Mentality-------------- 43
23. Practice, Practice, Practice---------------- 45
24. Chose To Be Happy----------------------- 47
25. Beat That Negative Habit----------------- 49
26. Offload Your Stress------------------------ 51
27. Seek Opportunities In Adversity--------- 53
28. Overcome Self-Deception---------------- 55
29. Learn From Your Own Mistakes--------- 57

30. Keep People's Secrets---------------------- 59
31. Manage Your Anger----------------------- 61
32. Never Abandon Your Dream-------------- 63
33. Do Not Be Too Hasty---------------------- 65
34. Protect And Pursue Your Vision---------- 67
35. Be Responsible For Your Life------------- 69
36. Avoid The Dangers of Flattery------------ 71
37. Do Not Try To Please Everyone----------- 73
38. Nurture Your Ideas------------------------ 75
39. Go After Your Goals----------------------- 77
40. Focus On Your Destination---------------- 79
41. Do Not Compare Yourself With Others--- 81
42. Look After Your Mind---------------------- 83
43. Let Go Of Obstructive Traditions---------- 85
44. Defend Yourself Correctly------------------ 87
45. Put the Past Behind you-------------------- 89
46. Develop Passion For All You Do----------- 91
47. Know Your Worth-------------------------- 93
48. Win The Three Dimensional Warfare----- 95
49. Keep Yourself Humble---------------------- 97
50. Confront Issues, Do Not------------------- 99
    Complain About Them
51. Overcome Insecurity-------------------------101
52. Spread Your Wings------------------------ 103

THE ORIGIN OF THIS BOOK

Several years ago, the Lord laid in my heart to begin writing daily devotionals to help enrich the spiritual lives of His people. It took a few more years before I actually commenced writing the first of what has now been going on for several years.

Many of the sections in this book have being gleaned from some of the writings of the daily devotionals which I broadcast electronically every day. A lot of people have encouraged me to put the writings in the form of a book both to preserve them and to make them accessible to a wider audience; this is the first in a series of books as a result the devotionals.

The book contains fifty-two short and easy-to-read chapters. They can be read one per day or one per week. You may find it interesting to read through them more than once in a year.

It is my prayer that you, like many people have, will find these short writings a blessing to your spiritual life. They are intended to be a source of inspiration, encouragement and spiritual enrichment to the reader, and I sincerely hope you will find them useful as you read from page to page.

Thank You.

Pastor Jerome Obode

One

LOOK AFTER YOURSELF

"Self-care is not selfish. You cannot serve from an empty vessel." – Unknown.

Many people are too concerned about being branded selfish, so they are continually under pressure to take care of others at the expense of their own welfare. Meanwhile, there is absolutely nothing wrong in looking after yourself, because by so doing you are better prepared, equipped and strengthened to serve others. Self-care is not selfish. You could end up putting those who depend on you at risk by not giving adequate attention to yourself.

Our greatest example, Jesus, rested Himself and His disciples. He once said to them: **"Come with me by yourselves to a quiet place and get some rest"** (Mark 6:31). Failure to look after your health could make you sick- you won't be able to care for your family and others who rely on you. Look after your emotional well-being- so you don't become edgy, angry and grumpy. **"Salt is good, but if it loses its saltiness, how can it be made salty again? It is fit neither** *for the soil nor for the manure pile; it is thrown out..."* (Luke 14:34-35).

There are several reasons why a lot of people put themselves last: They do not want to appear or be called selfish. Some people derive satisfaction from trying to meet everyone's needs, and feel guilty when they can't help. Others simply lack the power to say no, and usually have to over-explain themselves when they do. Having compassion towards people is essential, but it should not undermine self-compassion and self-respect. Striking a balance is particularly tricky for people who are kind-hearted, but Paul said, *"...no one ever hated his own body, but he feeds and cares for it, just as Christ does the Church- for we are members of His body* (Ephesians 5:29-30).

Be kind to yourself. Be kind to others. Be protective of your dreams. Bear in mind that you cannot effectively help others if you are hurting and struggling with issues. You can't save everyone. If you are overstretched you could end up getting bitter, harsh and antagonistic towards the same people for whom you have put yourself on the line. Remember that God loves a cheerful giver. For a lot of people, looking after themselves will take courage, discipline and putting a plan in place. We can only give out of our personal reservoir. If you are seriously 'depleted', you can't help others.

Two

LEAVE YOUR COMFORT ZONE

"A man grows most tired while standing still." – Chinese Proverb

A comfort zone is a familiar environment, a place where we feel at ease, unruffled and unchallenged. It is a place where nearly everything and everyone remains the same and we face no new challenges. When confronted with new challenges we get fearful, scared and tend to revolt. It is important you get out of your comfort zone because, *"The easy roads are crowded, and the level roads are jammed; the pleasant little rivers, with the drifting folk are crammed. But off yonder where it's rocky, where you get a better view, you will find the ranks are thinning, and the travellers are few."* - Unknown

The only way we can reach our full potential is to break free from our comfort bubble. **"For God has not given us a spirit of fear, but of power and of love and of a sound mind."** (2 Timothy 1:7). Most things that do not involve pain are less exciting and barely rewarding. Nothing of significance will happen until a person stretches and reaches out for the unfamiliar environment. Brian Tracy writes, "Move out of your comfort zone. You can only grow if you are willing to feel awkward and uncomfortable when you try something new." No one becomes what they want to be by remaining where they are. Form the habit of trying something new every time you begin to feel comfortable with where you are. ***"Have not I commanded thee? Be strong and of a good courage; be not afraid, neither be dismayed: for the LORD thy God is with thee whithersoever thou goest"*** (Joshua 1:9).

The things that we fear most usually hold the greatest blessings. The better life you crave for is located outside your familiar environment. People who remain in their comfort zones won't grow; and the absence of growth is an indication of gradual death. The comfort zone is a danger zone- it is a place for excuse makers, the visionless and people who are not desperate enough to risk anything for success. It is a place where dreams are buried. Every major victory begins at the end of the comfort zone. You will start to grow when you are ready to bear the discomfort and awkwardness that come with trying something new. Step out today and start doing those things that you are too scared to do.

Three

SEE YOURSELF ACCURATELY

"No one remains quite what he was, once he recognises himself"- Thomas Mann

There is the old story of a farmer who found an egg in an abandoned eagle's nest. He picked up the egg and added it to the eggs of a brooding hen. The egg hatched and the mother hen nurtured the eagle chick like she would her own chick. As the eagle grew up, it pecked, scratched, walked and lived like a chicken.

It happened one day that this eagle-chicken looked up at the sky and saw an eagle overhead, soaring majestically and effortlessly in the sky without restrain. Mesmerised by what she saw, the eagle asked, "What a magnificent bird!" "What is it?" The chicken neighbours replied, "That's an eagle – the king of birds," "But don't even dream about flying like that. You could never be like that." The eagle which has reached old age went back to live, eat, act and think like a chicken until his death.

How do you see yourself – a chicken or an eagle? Your answer to this question will determine what happens to you in life. Your identity determines your destiny. Your vision will determine your direction and acceleration in life. Seeing yourself accurately means seeing yourself the way God sees you. Do not try to conform to the images projected by TV, magazines, your neighbours or society. People's expectation should not define your life. ***"Do not conform any longer to the pattern of this world, but be transformed by the renewing of your mind"*** (Romans 12:2). What you see is what you get out of life. No amount of prayers or support will help a person who can only see failure, defeat, poverty and sickness.

You are who God says you are- saved, healthy, prosperous, an overcomer, wonderfully and fearfully made and able to do all things. God has loaded you with everything you ever wanted to become in life. You are God's special package to the world, a gift people are waiting to unwrap and discover God's unique blessings for their lives. This is the accurate picture. Nothing less! God's ***"... divine power has given to us all things that pertain to life and godliness, through the knowledge of Him who called us by glory and virtue..."*** (2 Peter 1:2-4). When you think accurately (in line with God's Word) of yourself, you will generate positive feelings and attract positive things to yourself.

Four

DEFINE YOUR OWN SUCCESS

"Finish whatever you begin, and experience the triumph of completion." Anonymous

American black reformer, Booker T. Washington, once said, "I have learned that success is to be measured not so much by the position one has reached in life as by the obstacles which one has overcome while trying to succeed."

Our environment, upbringing and preferred image contribute to the way we view success. Never adopt, or adapt to anyone's definition of success. What you call success is up to you. However, true success is only that which is rooted in God, and can stand for time and eternity. Some people are successful materially, but not in family and other relationships. Someone may be intellectually successful but have a very poor health or, are a moral failure. Many people have everything they need but are emotionally unstable.

For many people what matters most is effort, determination and satisfaction with what they do. Success is about doing what you can with what you have, starting where you are, and for as long as it takes- whatever the cost. Successful people are not only those who have completed the race, but those who continue until the race is over. Every step of progress is a step of success- so long as it is towards the direction of your dream.

True success is well-rounded; the Bible says, **"Beloved, I wish above all things that thou mayest prosper and be in health, even as thy soul prospereth."** (3John 1:2) God wants us completely successful materially, in receiving and giving love and enjoying good health. Being comfortable, knowledgeable and having a sound mind are part of success. Bigger does not always mean better. Let your aspirations be completely yours; achieve them, and if you can, in a big way. That is success!

"Though thy beginning was small, yet thy latter end should greatly increase." (Job 8:7). We see 'big successes' everywhere, but they all started small. Cherish and nourish your small beginning. We can never say we are truly successful until we live in total obedience to God. Think once again about your definition and perception of success- "Try not to become a man of success. Rather become a man of value."- Albert Einstein

Five

MAKE READING A HABIT

"A good book is the best of friends, the same today and forever." – Martin F. Tupper

The Bible says, **"Take hold of instruction; let her not go: keep her; for she is your life"** (Proverbs 4:13). Reading, learning, education (self or formal) takes you a step ahead of other people. People who fail to add to their knowledge and develop new skills continuously, will make themselves less and less valuable. Fresh knowledge is to you what fresh food, daily meals, nutritious diet is to your physical body. The day a person stops feeding, and feeding on the right food- they will start to deteriorate, and their physical strength will begin to wane.

To stay alive, strong and healthy physically, a person needs to be constantly nourished with the right food. Similarly, the right school is a great place to be, but more importantly, self-education is critical to self-development and excellence in life. **"A wise man will hear, and will increase learning; and a man of understanding shall attain unto wise counsels"** (Proverbs 1:5). A person who stops learning stops growing, stops making progress and would become less relevant.

When people say they do not have time to read, they are simply saying they do not want to read. Where you are today is the totality of the knowledge you gained over the years, and where you will be tomorrow will be a product of the books you read, the knowledge you accumulated and the skills you developed today. Anyone who does not embrace reading and learning will soon become irrelevant in today's world.

Everything we are or will ever be is connected to books- may be the ones read by our teachers, parents and trainers. Everything ever in existence is a product of books; someone may have had an original idea, but most ideas become perfected through books written by other people.
"No matter how busy you may think you are, you must find time for reading, or surrender yourself to self-chosen ignorance." - Confucius.

Let books be your dining table,
And you shall be full of delights
Let them be your mattress
And you shall sleep restful nights
    - Author Unknown

Six

SOW YOUR SEED

"...be not deceived; God is not mocked: for whatsoever a man soweth,

that shall he also reap" (Galatians 6:7).

The dictionary defines seed as "the beginning of something which continues to grow or develop"; "a source of development or growth". The Bible encourages the generous sowing of seed: *"In the morning sow thy seed, and in the evening withhold not thine hand: for thou knowest not whether shall prosper, either this or that, or whether they both shall be alike good"* (Ecclesiastes 11:6). Every seed carries the potential for multiplication. It is strange that too many people want to reap what they have not sown, they want a harvest where they have not planted.

Your seed could be anything God has endowed you with. God has blessed us with ideas, talents, skills, abilities and resources. We all have things that somebody somewhere craves for. Planting seasons are never easy, but failure to plant is even more painful. The answer to your need is in your seed, and a seed that is not planted has no chance of multiplication.

We will always reap what we sow. We reap after (not before) we sow; people who wait to have abundance or feel comfortable before they sow run the risk of never having a harvest. Many people become frustrated because they vaguely hope to harvest beautiful flowers where they have not planted flower-yielding seeds. Be careful what you eat, see, do or say today; it is a seed that will be harvested someday. Aim to plant seeds everywhere so you can reap everywhere. Aim to plant a seed into the life of everyone you meet daily, and very soon you will begin to reap where you have sown.

"Truly, truly, I say to you, unless a grain of wheat falls into the earth and dies, it remains alone; but if it dies, it bears much fruit" (John 12:24). Unless we sow our God-given talents and resources in the soil of people's lives, striving to become a blessing at every given opportunity, we will never be rewarded by our heavenly Father.

Preserve your seed. Plant your seed. Protect your seed, and watch out to see the wonders that will come out of them- even the tiniest seed has the potential of becoming a huge garden or a great forest. Give your seed a chance to become what God ordained it to be. Please, plant that seed today.

Seven

LET NOTHING STOP YOU

"There is nothing impossible to him who will try." - Alexander the Great

"A sound body, a brilliant mind, a cultural background, a huge amount of money, a wonderful education- none of these guarantee (sic) success. Booker T. Washington was born in slavery. Thomas Edison was deaf. Abraham Lincoln was born of illiterate parents... Robert Louis Stevenson had tuberculosis. Alexander Pope was hunchback. Admiral Nelson had only eye. Julius Caesar was an epileptic. But these men made history in spite of their handicaps. And there was Louis Pasteur, so near-sighted that he had a difficult time finding his way in laboratory without glasses. There was Helen who could not hear or see, who graduated with honours from a famous college." Source Unknown

Let nothing stop you. If you wait for things to be perfect you will never do anything. Never allow the devil to capitalise on your handicap- I mean limitations or weaknesses. Be they personal, economic, spiritual, geographical, educational or relational weaknesses, never let nothing stop you.

"No temptation has overtaken you that is not common to man. God is faithful, and he will not let you be tempted beyond your ability, but with the temptation He will also provide the way of escape, that you may be able to endure it." (1 Corinthians 10:13)

Turn your limitation over to God today, let Him take over every obstacle in your life and transform it into a miracle, let Him completely overhaul your life and make something beautiful out of it. He made the world out of nothing- in fact, from chaos. God can turn every problem into a beautifully finished product. He does not need a perfect you to give you the best- just abandon yourself in His hands and see what He will make out of you. God is an expert at bringing something good out of bad, sweet out of bitter and light out of darkness. He can flood a person's life with brightness in the midst of total darkness, so let nothing stop you.

God can make all things work out for your good if you will be courageous and not let your handicap stand in your way. He will make a way in the wilderness, rivers in the desert, if only you will hang on long enough to see His power move in your life.

Eight

LET GO OF THE TITANIC MENTALITY

"A single moment of understanding can flood a whole life with meaning." -Anonymous

The Titanic was a ship (first of its kind) considered unsinkable, but sank during her maiden voyage April 15, 1912 when an iceberg punctured it and caused it to sink into the bottom of the Atlantic Ocean. This led to the loss of over 1,500 lives. People erroneously believed that the ship was "practically unsinkable"; "The Captain may, by simply moving an electric switch, instantly close the doors throughout, and make the vessel practically unsinkable." Such was their confidence that the key rules and aspects of sailing in such a ship were ignored. The ship was capable of carrying 3,000 people, but had life boats that were far fewer than that- another cause for the huge loss of lives.

"Therefore, let him who thinks he stands take heed lest he fall." (1Corinthians 10:12)
God wants His children to be full of faith and confidence, but being overconfident can give rise to positive as well as negative consequences. Many people

have failed their exams because they were too relaxed and overly sure of themselves; rather than put in everything they could, they trusted in themselves and ended up with disappointments. Confidence and self-assurance have great benefits, but a know-it-all attitude can lead to the danger of self-delusion, procrastination and exaggerated belief in one self.

We should not live in fear and unbelief, but must also remember not to trust too much in ourselves; never assume things will always run smoothly. The safest thing is to trust in, and ask God daily for His abundant mercies in all aspects of our lives, even in those areas where we are well skilled and experienced.

The Bible says, *"...the race is not to the swift, nor the battle to the strong, neither yet bread to the wise, nor yet riches to men of understanding, nor yet favour to men of skill; but time and chance happeneth to them all."* (Ecclesiastes 9:11). Skills are important, knowledge is crucial, but it is best to rest our hearts in God as we let Him use the gifts and talents with which He has endowed us. We should work hard like everything depend on it, and train like it is the only requirement for success, but continue to recognise that whatever you do, God has the ultimate say in what happens in your life.

Nine

START YOUR DAY WITH GOD

"This is the day that the Lord has made; let us rejoice and be glad in it" (Psalm 118:24)

The discipline of rising early in the morning to pray or carry out important tasks has un-surpassing rewards. For many people, the ideal time to meet face to face with God is early in the morning. Although Jesus prayed at various times and in different places, He distinctively modelled the early morning prayers whilst He was on earth. *"And rising very early in the morning, while it was still dark, he departed and went out to a desolate place, and there he prayed" (Mark 1:35).*

No two days are the same, and you need God's help and guidance to tackle whatever each day throws at you. When you spend time praying early in the morning, committing your day to God, you will give Him a chance to breathe His life and power into your day. Spending time to study the Bible in the morning brings you God's Word for the day- a word from God in the morning will transform your day. Abraham rose early in the Morning (Genesis 19:27); Moses rose early in the morning (Exodus 24:4); Samuel's parents (Hannah and Elkannah) rose up early to worship the Lord (1 Samuel 1:19); Jesus rose up a great while before day to a solitary place to pray (Mark 1:35).

The importance of rising early to pray means the devil will do everything within his power to sabotage it. The Bible says, ***"Let me hear in the morning of your steadfast love, for in you I trust. Make me know the way I should go, for to you I lift my soul"*** (Psalm 143:8). If you are having difficulty rising early, try using more than one alarm clock (set at intervals) or enlist the help of a loved one to help you develop the habit. Remember the popular saying, 'no pain, no gain'. What can be more valuable than starting the day with our heavenly Father? It would make a world of difference to your life.

Waking up early at a specific time helps you to establish a routine that will enrich your quiet time with the Lord. Early rising will increase your productivity as you will have more time to accomplish your goals for the day. Rising early also helps to develop discipline.

Ten

AVOID PREJUDICE LIKE A PLAGUE

"Ignorance and prejudice are handmaidens of propaganda. Our mission, therefore, is to confront ignorance with knowledge, bigotry with tolerance, and isolation with outstretched hand of generosity. Racism can, will, and must be defeated."- Kofi Annan.

General Robert E. Lee was a devout follower of Jesus Christ. It is said that soon after the end of the American Civil War, he visited a church in Washington, D.C. During the communion service he knelt beside a black man. An onlooker said to him later, "How could you do that?" Lee replied, "My friend, all ground is level beneath the cross."- Source Unknown.

Prejudice originates from a root word that means to prejudge. It is easy to prejudge others and have misconceptions about them, without having enough grounds to do so. Prejudice can be extended to an individual, a race or a group of people. We become prejudiced if we 'box' people into a class or social status negatively, and then display unhealthy attitude towards them- overtly or covertly. God treats everyone equally, and so must we. *"For who maketh thee to differ from another? And what hast thou that*

thou didst receive? Now if thou didst receive it why dost thou glory, as if thou hadst not received it?" (1 Corinthians 4:7).

We can form a negative opinion about a group of people just because we have had some nasty experience with one or more individuals from that group. It is easy to become prejudiced towards people from a particular culture- the way they dress, eat, speak or even their social norms, simply because they dared to be different. God does not differentiate between people. ***"There is neither Jews nor Greek, there is neither bond nor free, there is neither male nor female: for ye are all one in Christ Jesus."*** (Galatians 3:28). It does not matter whether they are Christians or not, God expects us to love and relate with everyone equally. We are all God's creation.

Prejudice is a 'disease' which everyone must deal with deliberately. God expects His children to be able to accommodate what they do not like in others, and to display a dignified attitude towards them. God never made us different from others. There is nothing we are that is not by grace- beauty, riches, talents and opportunities. Whatever you are is a privilege. ***"Therefore all things whatsoever ye would that men should do to you, do ye even so to them: for this is the law and the prophets"*** (Matthew 7:12).

Eleven

KEEP GROWING SPIRITUALLY

"You are either becoming more like Christ every day or you are becoming less like Him. There is no neutral position in the Lord." -Stormie Omartin

There comes a point physically in our lives when we stop growing in certain areas. This is usually not the case when it comes to spiritual development. Spiritually, we never stop growing; fact is, God desires that we keep growing until we see Jesus face to face. Christian growth and maturity is not determined by how long we have been Christians, our gifting or spiritual environment. It is determined by how well a person has yielded to God.

Christian growth is not automatic; we have to work at it deliberately and continuously. Spiritual immaturity is one of the reasons many of God's children never truly enter into their God-ordained blessings. *"Now I say, that the heir, as long as he is a child, differeth nothing from a servant, though he be lord of all; But is under tutors and governors until the time appointed of the father. Even so we, when we were children, were in bondage under the elements of the world."* (Galatians 4:1-3).

We give incremental responsibilities to children based on how they meet their developmental milestones. In the same way, God releases His blessings to His children when they can demonstrate certain dimensions of maturity and responsibility. Your Christian life will only be as prosperous as your spiritual development. The Bible says, **"Beloved, I wish above all things that thou mayest prosper and be in health, even as thy soul prospereth."** (3 John 2). Some Christians never proceed beyond the infant stage of their relationship with God; with them life is all about receiving from God and being nursed by spiritual leaders; not about what they can give but can get. They still have to be nurtured over and again in their faith. Of such Christians Paul said, **"My little children, of whom I travail in birth again until Christ be formed in you... for I stand in doubt of you..."** (Galatians 4:19-20).

Many Christians want God to treat them like grownups, when, in fact, they still possess and exhibit all the traits of little children. God will not trust anyone with greater blessings or responsibilities until they can prove they are spiritually stable and reliable.

Twelve

ALWAYS DO MORE THAN IS REQUIRED

"Do all the good you can, by all the means you can..." Ralph Waldo Emerson

Oskar Schindler (1908-1974) was an ethnic German industrialist credited with saving 1,200 Jews (part of his 1,750 workforce) during World War 11, from the Holocaust. He saved them by employing them in his enamelware and ammunitions factories. Using his position, connection and influence, he systematically bought Jews to work in his ammunitions factory which produced ammunitions for Germany, in a bid to save them from destruction. He spent so much of his money buying Jews that by the end of the war he was literally financially bankrupt even though he entered the war as a wealthy industrialist.

As the war ended, Schindler told his Jewish employees they were free to go at midnight. He embraced one of them and crying, he said, "I could have done more". He looked at a few possessions he had left, and lamented that he could have bought more Jews with them, adding, "Why didn't I do more?"

Could you have done more for yourself last year? Could you have done more for neighbours and loved these past months and years? There is a lot more we can do for ourselves and humanity than we are currently doing. ***"...you know the grace of our Lord Jesus Christ that though He was rich, yet for your sake He became poor, so that you through His poverty might become rich" (2 Corinthians 8:9).*** Jesus gave us all He had. Many people sacrificed to bring the Gospel to us. Many of the benefits we enjoy today are the product of people's sweat and blood.

Mr Schindler gave everything he had; he risked his own life until he managed to save 1,200 lives. Life is short, and if we become too pre-occupied by our personal and family needs, we will never be able to accomplish much for God. We have opportunities every day to give our best to the world. We must give to the world, to everyone around us whatever blessings God can channel through us- we owe it to them.

Whatever it will take, we have a responsibility to overcome personal and external obstacles to become the greatest blessing we can to humanity. The Bible says we can do all things through Christ who gives us strength. You can do more, even if you have to start small.

Thirteen

KEEP ACCELERATING

"The secret of change is to focus all energy, not on fighting the old, but on building the new." - Socrates

A particular pilot described his early training, and his trainer's instruction as to the procedures that must be followed in an emergency. Regarding the throttle, flaps, engines, etc., he said, "Between each of them write on the card 'Fly the Airplane.'" He added that some years ago, a commercial airliner crashed in the swamps of Florida because the entire crew got so involved in the process of checking a landing gear which appeared not to be coming down, that they forget to keep flying the airplane.

When we stop moving, things will stop happening, and negative forces will start to gain influence. Always keep your momentum. Momentum is the fuel for motivation. Never lose sight of your worthwhile goal in the whirlwind of life. **"Let your eyes look directly forward, and your gaze be straight before you"** (Proverbs 4:25). No matter what life throws at you, keep pushing in the direction of your goals and objects; keep accelerating, and sustain momentum.

Anything that can slow your momentum can ultimately halt your progress and success.

Distraction and discouragement are twin enemies of progress. If you find yourself in a dead end, seek divine direction. God has promised: ***"I will instruct you and teach you in the way you should go; I will counsel you with my eye upon you"*** (Psalm 32:8). Keep dreaming and pursuing dreams; keep working for the Lord and on the things that matter most to you. Emergencies will always arise, challenges will never end, but the most important thing to do is to keep flying your airplane, and you will arrive at your destination in Jesus' name.

If the enemy cannot immediately stop you, He can gradually slow you down; and it's only a matter of time before things steadily ground to a halt. We cannot expect a car to move for long without pressing the acceleration pedal, or the savings account to keep growing without paying into it. Nor can we expect to maintain good health if we stop eating the right food and exercising.

Keep gaining and consolidating new ground. Stop taking frequent breaks. The next step is another one closer to your success, take it quickly- follow with another, and another without ever stopping. Things will not happen unless we make them to happen.

Fourteen

TAKE THE FIRST STEP

"Take the first step in faith. You don't have to see the whole staircase,

just take the first step."- Martin Luther King, JR

The first step is always very important. It may be little, scary and uncertain, but unless we take that initial step we cannot make progress. No matter how frightened you are about taking it, the moment you do, you will be on your way to success- out of stagnation, frustration, and dissatisfaction. If you take the first step God will see you through the rest of the journey because **"the steps of a good man are ordered by the LORD: and He delighteth in his way"** (Psalm 37:23).

Jeremiah knew that God has the power to bless and direct the steps we take: **"O LORD, I know that the way of man is not in himself: it is not in man that walketh to direct his steps"** (Jeremiah 10:23). Every first step is a step of faith; in many cases we may not know how the journey will go, or what lays ahead. However, the Lord says, **"When thou passeth through the waters, I will be with thee; and through the rivers, they shall not** *overflow thee; when thou walkest through fire, thou shall not be burned; neither shall the flame kindle upon thee"* (Isaiah 43:2).

Do not let past experiences hold you back. God has promised to do a new thing in your life, so try something new and see God do His work. (Isaiah 43:19). God said to Moses and the children of Israel to go forward when they were stranded by the Red Sea, awaiting the worst from their Egyptian enemies. God was aware that His people were terrified, unequipped and unprepared for an imminent attack from the Egyptians. But God knew what He would do to save His children- if only they would brave things and take some steps forward toward the Red Sea. (Exodus 14:15). Until the children of Israel took steps forward, God did not divide the Red Sea and make a way for them.

If we take small steps in the right direction, we may find out that the steps have ended up with big results. Even if you have to tip toe, wobble or even stumble, take the step anyhow- you never can tell where the journey will lead to, unless you dare to lift your foot.

Fifteen

RESLOVE TO WIN IN DIFFICULT TIMES

"Strength and growth come only through continuous effort and struggle." – Napoleon Hill

Charles K. Kettering stated, *"I could do nothing without problems, they toughen my mind. In fact I tell my assistants not to bring me their successes for they weaken me; but rather to bring me their problems, for they strengthen me."*

Everyone has troubles. Everyone goes through some form of hardship, they may not advertise them, but no body, not even the strongest or richest, is without their own challenges. Whatever you are facing in life, you will not be the first; millions are going through similar situations- certainly some people are going through even tougher times. What makes the difference between us all is that some people are more resilient than others, and this in all cases, will determine the outcome that we get.

Victory is sweetest and more valuable after we have successfully overcome struggles, challenges and obstacles. Great things never happen easily; easy ways rarely lead to greatness. God has promised to be our ever present help in times of trouble. ***"The LORD is a refuge for the oppressed, a stronghold in times of trouble. Those who know your name trust in you, for you, LORD, have never forsaken those who seek you"*** (Psalm 9:9-10). Every negative situation has some positives hidden in it. No situation is hopeless, so take every challenge as an adventure. Problems may bow you down, but never let them blow you up.

Challenges in your life are not there to destroy you; they are there to make you better, and help you realise your God-given potential. The real disaster is not in the problem itself, the greatest danger is in giving up. Difficulties do not destroy visions and dreams, they simply delay them. So you need all the patience and stamina from God to stay calm and strong until your dream unfolds. ***"Trust in the LORD with all thine heart, and lean not unto thine own understanding. In all thy ways acknowledge Him, and He shall direct thy paths"*** (Proverbs 3:5-6).

Never run away from problems, find a way around them. After all, stars shine the brightest when the night is darkest. Use your problems to develop your spiritual and emotional muscles, let them make you better at dealing with future challenges and leave behind great experiences and testimonies that will encourage people who are in similar situations.

Sixteen

GET RID OF THE 'LITTLE FOXES'

"Honesty is the best insurance policy." –
Brian Spellman

"Take us the foxes, the little foxes that spoil the vines: for our vines have tender grapes." (Song of Solomon 2:15). The fox is a skilful, clever and subtle animal belonging to the dog family. A fox is tricky, sly and clever; sneaky, destructive and evasive. Little foxes that spoil the vine are symbolic of little things that people do that could harm or devalue them. In the same way that little positive steps can generate outstanding results, so also can little mistakes, sins and seemingly harmless actions corrupt a person's life. The Bible says we should lay aside every weight and sin that easily beset us- in other words, we should deal with the little actions, attitudes and behaviours, including sin which stand in our way or cause us to be out of line with God (Hebrews 12:1).

Telling half-truth, taking office property without permission, gossip, little bits of un-forgiveness and bitterness, and occasionally watching sinful programmes on TV all make up the little foxes that can bring a person down. They may seem harmless, but can make a lasting impact on a person's life. The Bible says, ***"The integrity of the upright shall guide them: but the perverseness of the transgressor shall destroy them"*** (Proverbs 11:3).

The little foxes in a person's life may not actually be sins; they could simply be an area of vulnerability. It is very easy to underestimate their impact because their full force is never felt until it is too late. Everyone should identify their own little foxes and prayerfully get rid of them as quickly as possible. A mosquito may be very tiny, yet one bite from it can have such deadly consequences, that it can kill the strongest person on earth. One bite from sin, one silly mistake may be enough to ruin a life. Little mistakes have destroyed many great people even though they had overcome very big problems. Let go of the little foxes.

Little things do matter a lot. Every major achievement is a combination or an accumulation of tiny bits of action. It may never happen in one day, but doing things (negative or positive) long enough will yield massive outcomes which could either be destructive or life building. Anything that is not adding to a person's life is definitely taking away from it.

Seventeen

NEVER BETRAY PEOPLE'S TRUST

"To be trusted is a greater compliment than being loved" - George Macdonald

Relationships are built on mutual trust. Broken trust is often difficult to regain. Nobody is 100% trustworthy, only God is. The most reliable and dependable people in our lives are also capable of letting us down. People can change easily or over time. God never changes so we can rest on Him when people disappoint us. He says, **"... I am the LORD, I change not; therefore ye sons of Jacob are not consumed"** (Malachi 3:6). When there is a break down in trust, it does not always mean the other person is evil or has problems with you. It is probably because they are human, and have allowed their humanity to prevail.

Just as we expect others to be trustworthy, we also have a responsibility to be reliable and dependable. We should keep confidences, be loyal, consistent and keep promises. We must not walk out of people's lives when they need us the most. We shouldn't betray, or be dishonest to people who have faith in us. If someone has let you down, remember that **"It is better to**

trust in the LORD than to trust in princes" (Psalm 11:8). Anyone can fail but God will never. Because we are God's children we have everything it takes to be reliable. Someone may have disappointed you, but that doesn't mean you should be suspicious of everyone else. Let God count on you as a rock, pillar of support and a source of encouragement for people He sends your way. Make yourself trustworthy, let people know you for this, and let God bless you for it.

The following words are often used to describe a person who is worthy of trust: believable, credible, dependable, reliable, responsible, truthful, trustable, unfailing and honest. Do people associate us with some or all of these words? If so, keep it up and keep improving. If not, take steps to make adjustments. In addition to trusting others, we should learn to trust ourselves, but more than anything else we should place implicit trust in God.

If you find yourself in an environment where no want can be trusted, count yourself out, be a shining example so that our heavenly Father can be glorified through you. Trust people but keep your eyes open. Trust God, keep your eyes closed and go to sleep.

Eighteen

SURRENDER YOUR FEARS TO GOD

"Let me assert my firm belief that the only things we have to fear is fear itself."- Franklin D. Roosevelt

"Whatever you do, you need courage. Whatever course you decide upon, there is always someone to tell you that you are wrong. There are always difficulties arising that tempt you to believe your critics are right. To map out a course of action and follow it to an end requires some of the courage that a soldier needs. Peace has its victories, but it takes brave men and women to win them." – Ralph Waldo Emerson.

Fear is one of the greatest tools crafted by the devil to keep people from fulfilling their destiny. We can either face up to our fear, or simply give in to it. Fear is good when it stops you from doing wrong, breaking the law, staying out of danger and being complacent. Fear is bad when it impacts negatively on your success, progress, relationships and health. Build your life upon the Word of God and say to yourself, **"Though an army besiege me, my heart will not fear; though war break out against me, even then will I be confident"** (Psalm 27:3).

Set yourself free from fear by releasing control of your life to God. Failure is just another step towards success for those who keep trying. It is alright to be cautious in certain situations but, getting overcautious is a recipe for failure and future regrets. Be prepared to take risks and let God have His way. Give your fears to Him and your faith will rise. God's Word says, ***"The LORD Himself goes before you and will be with you; He will never leave nor forsake you. Do not be afraid; do not be dismayed"*** (Deuteronomy 31:8).

Everybody is afraid of something, but life has to continue in spite of fear, things have to be accomplished in the presence of fear. Fear has to be confronted face to face otherwise it will never turn back. If there was a person called fear, what would it feel like to find out one day that he is actually afraid of you- afraid that you will take the steps you need to take, that you will step into the dark to chase after your goal, and that you will never let anything stop you? Face your fears, confront them, start in small ways, and experience little wins and progress to bigger victories.

Nineteen

EMBRACE CHANGE

*"Determination, patience and courage are the only things needed
To improve a situation. And, if you want a situation changed badly enough, you will find these three things."- Anonymous*

Not many people like to hear the word change, especially if it involves a major disruption and discomfort to their lives. The kind of change that will dramatically alter the course of an individual's life will, in many cases, involve a relative amount of pain and irritation. But the good news is that the payback from change far outweighs the initial awkwardness and anxiety that come with it.

"For everything there is a season, and a time for every matter under heaven." (Ecclesiastes 3:1). If we fail to change at the right time, we stand to lose the full benefits associated with that particular change. Our personality, background, mental toughness, and faith combine to determine how we respond to any adjustment we need to make. If we really want a new direction for our lives, then we should not be afraid to go through the inconvenience

that goes with it. We can simply chose to resist, tolerate or altogether embrace change. The third option is the best.

Until we feel comfortable making changes whenever it is needful, we are unlikely to get the most out of life. Everyone knows where they need to improve, but few possess the courage and discipline to start or see things through. We can never change everything, but we can start from somewhere. The only way out of where we are, out of what we don't like, is to change what needs to be changed. Many situations in our life will remain the same until we are happy to embrace change.

Every form of innovation and invention is usually preceded by a process of change. Anyone who fails to alter their attitude towards change will hardly experience something new in their life. Change- constant change- no matter how uneasy and unsettling it may be, is the only route to the next level of growth and glory.

No matter how well you are doing in an area, there is always a need to do something differently and that will involve change. If we fail to change the direction we are currently heading, we will end up exactly there: for some people, that will be disastrous; for others, it will be mediocrity; and for the last group, it will be failure to maximise their potential.

Twenty

NEVER FEAR YOUR CRITTICS

"Critics are our friends, they show us our faults."
– Benjamin franklin

"If I tried to answer all the criticisms of me and all the attacks levelled at me, this office would be closed to all other business. My job is not pleasing men, but doing the best I can. If in the end I am found to be wrong, ten legions of angels swearing I was right will not help me; but if the end proves me to have been right, then all that is said about me now will amount to nothing."- Abraham Lincoln

There is only one group of people in the world who are insulated from critics- those who say nothing, do nothing and become nothing. To be afraid of critics or criticism is to be *afraid* of making progress. To criticise is easy, but accepting criticism is not easy, so before you criticise, ask yourself if you were the object of that criticism, how would you feel? Some people criticise out of self-righteousness. Some criticise out of malice. Very few people criticise constructively, out of care and love. We have to be careful which of these categories we fall into.

What do we do when we are criticised? Criticism hurts, and is often difficult to accept. When received with humility and an open heart, we can reap the benefits of criticism. Jesus says, **"...Let your light so shine before men, that they may see your good works, and glorify your father which is in heaven"** (Matthew 5:16). Shine the light of love, truthfulness, honesty, fairness and hard work whenever people criticise or try to pull you down. And, to habitual critics, whatever they sow they will reap- it is God's law. If you are being criticised, accept what is true, act upon it; it will make you better.

Most critics are jealous and angry people, and why would I let such a person dampen my enthusiasm, why would I be afraid to do something just because some people will derive pleasure in running me down when they have not walked a mile in my shoes? Most critics are onlookers and spectators who are yet to do something worthwhile for their generation. If anyone is overly and harshly critical of your accomplishment, look very well to see what and how well they have achieved in that area. If you feel they are genuine, embrace their advice, if not discard with it.

Twenty One

LOOK AFTER YOUR HEALTH

"Health and cheerfulness mutually beget each other." – Joseph Addison

Isaak Walton said, *"Look after your health; and if you have it, praise God, and value it next to a good conscience; for health is the second blessing that we mortals are capable of; a blessing that money cannot buy."*

Nothing in the world can compare with good health. You do not need perfect health to reach your goals in life, but you do need good health to be able to do a lot of things to the best of your ability. It is God's desire for His people to enjoy perfect health: ***"Beloved, I wish above all things that thou mayest prosper and be in good health, even as thy soul prospereth"*** (3rd John 2). Given the same talents, resources and opportunities, a healthy person will outperform someone whose health is poor. In the absence of sudden and unfortunate events, a healthy person will outlive someone who does not enjoy good health.

With good health you can go as far as you really want with your goals; you will feel better and happier within you. In the event that you are not enjoying good health, God has made provisions in His Word for the healing of His people. Jesus came to save us from sin and sickness. ***"... His own self bare our sins in His own body on the tree that we, being dead to sins, should live unto righteousness: by whose stripes ye were healed."*** (1 Peter 2:24).

It is critical that we protect our health jealously, and take appropriate steps to stay healthy and fit. Good food, proper rest, sensible and continuous exercise are very critical to enjoying good health. Many people will squander their health in search of wealth, but in reality there is no true wealth in the absence of good health.

Staying healthy will help you live longer, perform better and become the best you want to be. Protect your health by all means, because in most cases when it's gone, it's gone. Go for regular health checks, exercise and look after your mental health. Use the dentist, doctor and optician; they are there for a reason. Many things in life can be replaced, but not health- one of the greatest things you owe yourself is to stay fit and healthy- you need it more than anything else the world can provide.

Twenty Two

REJECT THE VICTIM MENTALITY

"Resist the temptation to see yourself as a victim." – James Dobson

A victim is someone who has suffered harm. A victim mentality is a learned state in which an individual habitually thinks as a victim of other people's negative actions. Victim mentality makes a person think and act like others are responsible for what they suffer, even when there is no evidence to prove so.

It is a mind-set that makes a person feel powerless, shirk responsibility and avoid risk taking. It puts an individual in a kind of bondage whereby they are unable to live happy and fulfilled lives. The Bible says, *"It is for freedom that Christ has set us free, Stand firm, then, and do not let yourselves be burdened again by a yoke of slavery"* (Galatians 5:1). Never let your history stand in your way; you have the power to change and shape your life. A victim mentality traps a person in the status quo, and drains them of the spirit of happiness. People who feel like victims hold themselves back ever before (if at all) anyone else does.

The victim's state of mind is often characterised by fear. Fear stops us from fulfilling God's plans for our lives. The Bible says, ***"Do not fear, for I am with you; do not be dismayed, for I am your God. I will strengthen you and help you; I will uphold you with my righteous right hand"*** (Isaiah 41:10). When we begin to take responsibility, we will stop blaming our parents, early childhood, boss, society and friends for our negative experiences- past or present, and we will be able to say, ***"I can do all things through Christ who strengthens me"*** (Philippians 4.:13). The victim mentality is a self-inflicted state for which the sufferer needs self-deliverance as it leads to mediocrity, irresponsibility, and failure.

Make up your mind today to go for the life you always wanted, refuse to be a victim of circumstances; shake off every self-defeating belief because life is not kind to self-made victims. Start looking inward for solutions because God has blessed you with them; let the king inside you begin to reign on the throne of your life. The world is not responsible for shaping your life, you are responsible for shaping the world. Let the light within you start to shine; hand your mind over to God and let Him uproot every seed of loneliness, hopelessness and worthlessness.

Twenty Three

PRACTICE, PRACTICE, PRACTICE

"The difference between ordinary and extra ordinary is practice." – Vladimin Horowite

An ordinary person can do extra ordinary things if they apply themselves and practice until they excel in a particular area. Everybody wants to change something, achieve a goal or have some new experience, but too many people seem to believe that more time, knowledge and resources are what they need to help them in the achievement of their goals. Additional information is important, but utilising what we already know is more important than more information. Whatever the goal- learning a new language, writing a book, eating healthier, saving more money or losing weight, continuous practice will yield better results than continuous learning without corresponding massive action.

"Nothing good comes in life or athletics unless a lot of hard work has preceded the effort. Only temporary success is achieved by taking short cuts." - Roger Staubach. Paul wrote to the Philippian Christians: **"Whatever you have learned or received or heard from me, or seen in me- put it into**

practice. And the God of peace will be with you" (Philippians 4:9). No one can expect God to move in their lives unless they are actively taking steps in the right direction. Anything can be mastered through relentless practice. We can prosper in whatever we do if have the courage to keep doing it until it becomes second nature.

Forgiveness, love, holiness, effective prayer and obedience to God can all be mastered through adequate exercise. Happiness, positive thinking and confession, networking and public speaking can be mastered through long term practice. We can train ourselves to speak fewer words, meet deadlines, keep our word and be an example of punctuality. Paul said to Timothy, ***"Do not neglect the gift you have, which was given you by prophecy when the council of elders laid their hands on you"*** (1 Timothy 4:14). He encouraged Timothy to use the gifts he already had, so he can excel in his role.

The main obstacle to goal achievement is the absence of practice. Repetition and reinforcement will give you the competitive edge in whatever you set out to do. We should not only practice until we get things right, we must practice until we no longer get things wrong. If you practice sufficiently it will result in efficiency and improved productivity. Aim to be the best. Aim to be the best through deliberate and continuous practice. Do not stop practicing even when you think you have arrived.

Twenty Four

CHOSE TO BE HAPPY

"It is not how much we have, but how much we enjoy, that makes happiness."- Charles Spurgeon

Once when recruiting for 500 employees to fill positions for a new facility, a hotel chain interviewed 5,000 people. The team carrying out the interview eliminated candidates who smiled less than four times during the interview. This criterion applied to interviewees in all job categories.

Your happiness should not depend on anything or anybody; if it does it will not last, because people and things can change at any time. Lasting happiness is a gift from God. Jesus is God's special gift to the world. True happiness can only come from knowing Him, and serving Him by serving others. **"As each has received a gift, use it to serve one another, as good stewards of God's varied grace."** (1 Peter 4:10). A life that is poured out on others can never run out of joy. The more we live for others the happier we will be.

No one can make you permanently joyful. Favours, gifts and success will attract temporary happiness. To enjoy lasting happiness you have to be ready to serve others and pour yourself into people, accept who you are and see yourself the way God sees you. Success will not make a person happy, but happiness can lead to success. Stop taking failures and other challenges too seriously- they won't kill you- they haven't these past years. Comparing yourself with others only makes you feel inferior, afraid and worthless, and it is pointless. Learn to celebrate who you are and the little strides you have made. You have enough within and around you to make you happy. To be happy, you have to go for it, not in things, but from within. And no one can make you unhappy unless you give it up.

Choose to be happy, never let go of it, no matter what happens. You owe it to yourself. When we live in obedience to God's Word, we are on the path to true happiness. This may not happen every moment, but Jesus has guaranteed our happiness through the Holy Spirit: ***"He that believeth on me, as the scripture hath said, out of his belly shall flow rivers of living waters"*** (John 7:38). Do not wait for everything to be positive, look for the positives in everything. Love and celebrate who you are, that is the foundation of satisfaction in life.

Twenty Five

BEAT THAT NEGATIVE HABIT

"Habit is habit, and not to be flung out the window by man, but coaxed downstairs, a step at a time"
Mark Twain

"No temptation has seized you except what is common to man. And God is faithful; He will not let you be tempted beyond what you can bear. But when you are tempted, He will also provide a way out so that you can stand up under it." (1 Corinthians 10:13 NIV)

An elderly teacher took with him one of his pupils on a walk through the forest. The teacher stopped, pointing to four plants nearby, he asked the pupil to carry out some exercises which involved four plants. The first plant was only beginning to sprout above the soil, the second had been fairly rooted; the third a shrub; the fourth was a mature tree.

The teacher instructed the learner to pull up the first plant. Effortlessly the youngster did so. 'Now pull up the second', said the teacher. The young person did with more effort. The teacher then instructed, 'Pull up the third plant.' The boy did, but had to expend all his energy. 'Now,' the teacher said, 'have a go at the fourth.' As hard as he tried, he could not even shake the tree or its leaves. The teacher replied, 'Son, this is the way our bad habits work. In the early stages, we can easily get rid of them; but when they are well formed, it is difficult to uproot them no matter how hard we work at it.'

Habits are behaviour patterns developed by recurrent practice. Our habits reflect our character. Temporarily they may provide some levels of comfort or pleasure, but often time, when they become ingrained, bad habits are difficult to change. Equally, good habits can permanently become the engine of an individual's progress. The Bible says, ***"Everything is permissible for me – but not everything is beneficial. Everything is permissible for me – but I will not be mastered by anything" (1 Corinthians 6:12).*** Christ has set us free, and He does not want us to be slaves to anything. We should continue to enjoy the liberty God has given us. ***"… for a man is slave to whatever has mastered him." (2 Peter 2:19).*** Anyone can change negative and unproductive habits by yielding completely to, and relying on God. We were not born with self-sabotaging habits, we learned them after birth; we can also unlearn them with a little more effort.

Twenty Six

OFF LOAD YOUR STRESS

"Anxiety does not take away stress; it just enhances it." – Debasish Mridha

Many cases of stress are the result of taking on excessive or unnecessary burden. Giving room to stress can be very expensive. Too much stress can lead to loss of energy, direction and discretion. Some people respond positively to stress by becoming more motivated and productive. Others react negatively and experience physical symptoms such as too much or little sleep, stomach ulcers, headaches, loss of concentration and inability to make decisions. God's Word says, **"Cast your burden on the LORD, and he will sustain you; he will never permit the righteous to be moved"** (Psalm 55:22).

Sometimes we need to go slow to go fast. A lot of times, speed and quantity will fail, but slow and steady will win the race. Some people become stressed because they failed to finish what they started, other times it is because they have bitten more than they can chew or have set expectations that are too high. John Newton advised, "We can easily manage if we will only take, each day, the burden appointed to it. But the load will be too heavy for us if we carry yesterday's burden over again today, and then add the burden of the morrow before we are required to bear it."

We can manage stress by not taking on too much, taking breaks away from work and home on a regular basis, and through regular exercise. Above all, staying close to God is the master key for reducing stress. ***"Except the LORD build the house, they labour in vain that build it: except the LORD keep the city, the watchman waketh but in vain"*** (Psalm 127:1-2). Unfortunately, a lot of people disconnect from God and spiritual activities when they are overcome by stress.

You may need to speak to an expert such as a counsellor or therapist with the professional knowledge and skills to support you if you are unable to manage or cope with things. Generally, stress can act as booster to achievement in some people; in others, it can cause a lot of damage. Through wisdom and tapping into God's power, we can effectively manage any type of stress. Taking adequate rest will help relieve you of stress. Learn not to overreact to stressful situations; our reaction to difficult times can sometimes be our undoing.

Twenty Seven

SEEK OPPORTUNITIES IN ADVERSITY

"If the road is easy, you're likely going in the wrong way." – Gordon B. Hinckley.

"What really makes people satisfied with their lives? Amazingly, the secret may lie in a person's ability to handle life's blows without blame or bitterness. These are the conclusions of a study of 173 men who have been followed since they graduated from Harvard University in the early 1940s. The study, reported in the American Journal of Psychiatry, noted that one potent predictor of well-being was the ability to handle emotional crisis maturely."- Today in the Word, November 2, 1993.

When Satan throws everything at you and you become overwhelmed with crisis, that is the time to prove the 'stuff' you are made of as a Christian. In the day of adversity receive God's power to turn your stumbling blocks into building blocks. Job, a man who experienced unparalleled and cataclysmic events, said: **"But He knows the way that I take; when He has tested me, I shall come forth as gold"** (Job 23:10). Challenges are inevitable in life. Job went through uncommon crisis. Yet, **"In all this, Job**

sinned not, nor charged God foolishly." (Job 1:22).

Life is like a bumpy bus ride, and sometimes like bumpy, scary flight. But with God's hands underneath you, all you will feel is the bumps if you simply rest your heart in God and keep hanging in. Never stop trying until there is a turnaround in your situation. No matter what you face, just hold on tight to your dreams and the Lord. Until you let go, nothing can stop you from realising your dream. Give your situation some more time. Habakkuk said: ***"Although the fig tree shall not blossom, neither shall fruit be in the vines; the labour of the olives shall fail ... yet I will rejoice in the LORD, I will joy in the God of my salvation"*** (Habakkuk 3:17-18).

Find a reason to be happy, prayerful and optimistic. Stay around people who can inspire and encourage you. Never fail to look for the hidden opportunity within your challenges. Hardships either make or break a person. Problems will challenge your creativity, ability and tenacity. Crisis will give you an opportunity to demonstrate God's power and prove your adversaries wrong. Fernando Sabino says it well, "In the end, everything will be okay. If it's not okay, it's not yet the end."

Twenty Eight

OVERCOME SELF-DECEPTION

"A mask can hide you from others, but not from yourself." – Marty Rubin

In a business scheme that ultimately shattered her dream, a school teacher lost her life savings to a very convincing swindler. Thereafter, she went for professional advice and help. "Why on earth didn't you come to us first?" An official asked. The lady replied, "I've always known you existed. But I didn't come because I was afraid you'd tell me not to do it."

Too often people know in their heart they are on the wrong path but still lie to themselves that all is well. The Bible says, *"For the time will come when they will not endure sound doctrine; but after their own lusts shall they heap to themselves teachers, having itching ears; And they shall turn away their ears from the truth, and shall be turned unto fables."* (2 Timothy 4:3-4). Even in the Church today, there is plenty of self-deception. God says, *"The prophets prophesy falsely, And the priests rule on their own authority; And My people love it so..."* (Jeremiah 5:31). There is plenty of gimmick and 'magic' going on but people pretend not to know.

Self-deception can lead to avoidance of truth, hoping a negative habit will disappear without working at it, and expecting personal debts to be wiped off without a strict plan. Self-delusion involves brushing things under the carpet instead of confronting them. Self-deceit results in self-denial, self-defence and day dreaming. It is bad enough to lie to others, but it is a dangerous thing to lie to ourselves. Only a few things will harm a person's success more than lying to themselves. We may hide the truth from people using all forms of vices, but we should be willing to face up to the truth we know about ourselves.

A. W. Tozer explains it better: "Of all forms of deception, self-deception is the most deadly, and of all deceived persons the self-deceived are the least likely to discover the fraud." Everyone knows the ways in which they have been deceiving themselves; they are the only ones that can do something about it. Being honest with ourselves is the only path to growth and prosperity. Most of the solutions for failure of any nature, lie within us. When people stop expecting mere wishes to become reality, they will begin to discover the way out of self-made obstacles. "Self-deception is the surest way to self-destruction. Reality has a way of catching up with us."- Sam Erwin

Twenty Nine

ALWAYS LEARN FROM YOUR MISTAKES

"Anyone who has never made a mistake has never tried anything new." – Albert Einstein

Mistakes are part of everyday life, but unfortunately we are all scared of making them because people are generally intolerant of other peoples' errors. We get embarrassed, stigmatised and sometimes rejected because we have faltered in certain areas. Nobody takes pride in making mistakes, but we can be proud of the lessons learned from them. The only people who do not get things wrong are those who never try anything worthwhile. How we made a mistake is one thing, but how we handle them is more important- this is what defines us.

As there are no perfect people or situations, we can never avoid making mistakes altogether. People who keep trying, keep making mistakes are far better than those who are too afraid to try, too scared to make mistakes and end up achieving nothing. There is no greater teacher than a mistake, so go after your dream aggressively.

When you know what you want to do, go for it. Defeat, disappointments and despair can be used by God to bring us into our promised land. Tell your doubters and those who laugh at you, **"Rejoice not over me, O my enemy; when I fall, I shall rise; when I sit in darkness, the LORD will be a light to me"** (Micah 7:8). We learn a lot more from failure than we can from success; however, we must aim not to make the same mistakes repeatedly. If you fall, God **"... will deliver you from six troubles; in seven no evil shall touch you"** (Job 5:19). We also have a responsibility to bear with others when they get things wrong. It does not mean they are evil or cannot be trusted; neither does it mean they are a failure- we have to be ready to give them more chances even if they keep disappointing.

You may struggle in life, but never let your struggles define you; you will continue to make mistakes, but never let the mistakes discourage you. You are who God's says you are. The skills, wisdom and knowledge to make good judgment today come from experience, and past mistakes form a major part of that experience. Learn from your own mistakes; also be prepared to learn from the mistakes of others. Today's error is tomorrow's lesson; only pray that you do not continue to make the same mistakes over and again.

Thirty

KEEP PEOPLE'S SECRETS

"Most of us can keep a secret. It's the people we tell it to who can't." - Unknown

Learning to keep confidences is a sign of maturity and integrity. People confide in us because they believe we are trustworthy. Not all secrets are bad, so we must learn to keep secrets except if doing so will greatly harm someone else or make us break the law. Ability to keep secrets is a litmus test of true strength of character. Secrets are golden. For how long should we keep them? For as long as we are expected to! The formulas for making Coca-Cola and Kentucky Fried Chicken still remain secrets; people have made this happen.

Jesus kept some things secret, and instructed certain people to leave it that way- at least for a period of time: **"...But when Jesus knew it, He withdrew Himself from thence: and great multitudes followed Him, and He healed them all; And charged them that they should not make Him known"** (Matthew 12:15-16). Faithful and loyal people never disclose confidential information. It is a sad thing that many people will reveal secrets for personal gains. It may be ethical to reveal a secret if other people will be seriously harmed by not speaking out. If we cannot keep people's secrets they will never entrust us with special information- this can affect healthy relationships, including work relationships.

We should not hold back information in order to cover up sins or wrong doings, ***"Neither be partaker of other men's sins"*** (1 Timothy 5:22). Some information are better concealed, but not if doing so will make us deceitful to our loved ones, employer, or break someone's heart when they find out. The best way to live is to stay honest and never do anything that will be embarrassing should anyone find out.

A secret is not worth keeping if it will seriously harm other people- except if the benefits far outweigh the cost, for example in the interest of national security. God desires truth at all times. ***"Beware, lest ye also, being led away with the error of the wicked, fall from your own steadfastness"*** (2 Peter 3:17). Remember also that we cannot hide things from God, He sees and knows everything, even the best kept secrets. It hurts to reveal other people's secrets. It is usually unwise to do so as it can break down trust and friendships. If we are privileged to gain access to people's restricted information, we have a responsibility to keep them to ourselves.

Thirty One

MANAGE YOUR ANGER

"Anger is just one letter short of danger" - Unknown

"Anger ... it's a paralyzing emotion ... you can't get anything done. People sort of think it's an interesting, passionate, and igniting feeling — I don't think it's any of that — it's helpless ... it's absence of control — and I need all of my skills, all of the control, all of my powers ... and anger doesn't provide any of that — I have no use for it whatsoever." – Unknown source

Anger is an intense feeling of displeasure towards something or somebody. Anger can be used in both positive and negative ways. Unfortunately, many people prefer to harvest the negative fruit of anger. It is hard to find anyone who never gets angry. Being angry is not the greatest problem, but doing so at the right time, correctly and without overdoing it, is where the challenge lies. ***"Be not hasty in thy spirit to be angry: for anger resteth in the bosom of fools."*** (Ecclesiastes 7:9). Uncontrolled anger can lead to bad judgement, embarrassment, lost opportunities, shame and regrets. ***"He that hath no rule over his own***

spirit is like a city that is broken down, and without walls." (Proverbs 25:28).

It is best to control your temper, if not you could find yourself making unbelievable and embarrassing mistakes, and running into all sorts of problems. A calm response in a heated situation can help the other person 'cool off'. It doesn't mean you are weak or fearful; it does mean you are skillful, mature and self-controlled. A Chinese proverb says: *"If you are patient in one moment of anger, you escape a hundred days of sorrow."*

Anger does not reflect power, it can be a sign of weakness. It does not win you respect, it can damage your reputation. Each time a person loses their temper, they will almost certainly lose something else. When out of control, anger can lead to shame, pain and disgrace. The price of anger can range from an accident, a jail term, a damaged relationship to lost opportunities. It does not only hurt the person to whom it is directed, there is always likelihood that an angry person will reap greater consequences from failing to manage it. Have you ever lost anything to uncontrolled anger? Always strive to hold back, we all have what it takes to stop anger from turning into hostility.

Thirty Two

NEVER ABANDON YOUR DREAM

"You are what you do, not what you say you'll do" – C.G Jung

Your dream is that imaginary picture you want to see materialise. It is your cherished aspiration, ambition or things you desperately want to achieve. Dreams never come true unless they are pursued. Many dreams remain unrealised because people take too long to prepare before going after them. There are times when we actually need to start walking before we are ready, and continue to learn along the way. We will never achieve anything just by dreaming; dreams will remain what they are- just dreams, unless we embrace the unknown, look fear in the eye and confront our limitations.

Your dream may be writing a book, learning a new skill, starting a business or some charity work. It could be doing a PhD, losing weight or overcoming a negative habit. It all takes courage; yes, you may fall, sustain bruises, or probably give up for some time. It is like learning to walk as a child. No matter what the fears were, you kept walking until you could run, skip, jump and dance- all by yourself. You need that same level of bravery and determination to make your dream come true. The Lord told Joshua: ***"Have not I commanded thee? Be strong and of a good courage; be not afraid, neither be thou dismayed: for the LORD thy God is with thee withersoever thou goest."*** (Joshua 1:9)

Are you thinking of stepping out into a new and uncharted territory? Are you contemplating doing something notable for yourself, your family or for God? Theodore Roosevelt said: *"Far better it is to dare mighty things, to win glorious triumphs, even though checkered by failure, than to rank with those poor spirits who neither enjoy much nor suffer much, because they live in the grey twilight that knows neither victory nor defeat."*

A dream that is not acted upon is only a fantasy. Love your dream, talk your dream, walk your dream- but above all work daily on your dream. The perfect time to pursue you dream will never come, so don't wait for it. Ignore those who tell you it can't happen, you do not need them; surround yourself with people who believe in your dream; shut out the dream killers from your life. Every dream takes time, a bigger dream may take a longer time, but never give up because dreams do come true.

Thirty Three

DO NOT BE TOO HASTY

"Rashness succeeds often, still more often fails."- Napoleon Bonaparte

We all have a tendency to do things in a hurry without slowing down to think. We should act with speed in whatever we do and in many cases; reluctance is a recipe for failure and a squanderer of opportunities. It is better to make quick decisions and some errors than to make no decisions, no mistakes and no progress. However, an over eagerness to act can lead to irreparable mistakes. Acting rashly is unwise, reckless and may not yield desirable outcome. Someone said, *"take time for all things: great haste makes great waste."* – Benjamin Franklin

Hastiness can lead us into saying or doing things we will later regret. When we reply before understanding what the other person has to say, jump into conclusion about people's actions, react badly to another driver when driving, it is a sign that we need some more lessons in patience. **"He that hath no rule over his own spirit is like a city that is broken down, and without walls" (Proverbs 25:28),** and **"He that is slow to wrath is of great understanding; but he that is hasty of spirit exalteth folly"** (Proverbs 14:29). Unreasonable haste is an express way to unnecessary pain. Speed is a critical element for personal and business success, but hurrying without due thought, to make things happen, can lead to terrible failure.

We need speed in so many areas of life, we equally need to calm down and weigh the cost against the benefits of anything we set out to do. It is important to look back and ask ourselves how many decisions we have made hurriedly in the past and what impact they had on us and our loved ones. It is alright to forgive in a hurry, race after an opportunity, hurry to return a kind gesture, but we should weigh the consequences of hasting to make promises, throwing aside caution when making an investment and making decisions that will impact greatly on us and the people around us.

Too much haste can cause a person to stumble. Life is a Marathon not a sprint. I have watched many athletes run long races, and carefully observed that the first three or four fastest – those who lead from the starting point are (in many cases) not usually the winners. Benjamin Franklin said, "Reckless haste makes a poor speed."

Thirty Four

PROTECT AND PURSUE YOUR VISION

"Vision without guts is fantasy" **Toba Beta**

Bob Logan described vision as:
"The capacity to create a compelling picture of the desired state of affairs that inspires people to respond; that which is desirable, which could be, should be; that which is attainable. A godly vision promotes faith rather than fear. A godly vision motivates people to action. A godly vision requires risk-taking. A godly vision glorifies God, not people."

Your vision is the key to your future. **"Where there is no vision, the people perish...."** (Proverbs 29:18). What you see is what you get. The direction and speed of your life is determined by what you see, and how your life will end. Paul prayed that, **"The eyes of your understanding being enlightened; that ye may know what the hope of His calling is, and what the riches of the glory of his inheritance in the saints..."** (Ephesians 1:18). Money and opportunities are not our greatest needs; if we can see clearly we will find a way round every obstacle.

Vision can come in the form of inspiration, revelation, a prompt, or a strong feeling towards a certain direction. A person may be physically blind, and yet see great things that others do not see. A future that is not seen will never be lived. There are many things we need to see that we do not see at all, and there are many things we need to see that we only see partially. When driving in the rain you need windscreen wipers; when it is foggy, you need the fog lights; to see as far as God will like you to see, ask for the Spirit's cleansing and inspiration- He is the Spirit of truth. He will show you the way out of the woods. If you can see great things, you will do great things.

Vision that is not coupled with action will lead to nowhere; action that lacks vision can make a person run in circles; vision coupled with action is a game changer- it will not only transform your life, it will make you an agent of change- you will break grounds, create opportunities and bring great blessings to many people wherever you go. What is your vision? You definitely need one- a compelling one that will grip you so much that nothing in the world will be able to stop you.

Thirty Five

BE RESPONSIBLE FOR YOR LIFE

***"The price of greatness is responsibility."* – Winston Churchill**

In today's world, few people want to take responsibility for their own lives. We blame the drinks industry for too much sugar that makes us unhealthy. We blame the government for not doing enough to help us get rich. We blame the examiner for making the exams too hard rather than our failure to work hard to pass the exams. We blame parents for an early childhood which we believe is responsible for our present struggles. We criticise our employers for everything that goes wrong at the place of work without striving to offer solutions to the problems.

Everybody is accusing somebody for every malady and no one is ready to take responsibility. It is easy to blame the computer, traffic and colleagues for doing things late. Habitually blaming others perpetuates failure and defeat. The Bible says, **"He that covereth his sins shall not prosper: but who so confesseth and forsaketh them shall have mercy."** (Proverbs 28:13). We become better by finding solutions rather than finding excuses. If we keep laying the blame somewhere, we may find it difficult to get on with our life; making progress will become impossible.

Accusing others blindfolds us from examining ourselves; it may offer temporal relief but very soon we will find that it robs us of creativity and our God-given ability. You can only enjoy true freedom if you develop the habit of looking inward, going forward, and understanding that finding excuses will lead nowhere. Steve Maraboli said: "We may place blame, give reasons, and even have excuses, but in the end, it is an act of cowardice to not follow your dreams." Lousi Nizer added: "When a man points a finger at someone else, he should remember that four of his fingers are pointing at himself."

We should admit that we were angry- not that someone made us angry. We should accept that we are late- not that the traffic was responsible. We should own up about not loving and caring enough for our spouse- not that he or she is such an impossible person. We should take up the challenge of learning new skills and stop blaming the economy for not producing jobs that align with our current skills.

Thirty Six

AVOID THE DANGERS OF FLATTERY

"Knavery and flattery are blood relations." – Abraham Lincoln

To flatter means giving excessive or insincere praise to somebody. It paints a wrong and dishonest picture of someone else. It involves papering over another person to present an image that is different from reality- making someone feel or look better than they should be. A flatterer gives a false but seemingly positive impression of someone they fear or respect; they may also flatter for their own selfish interest.

Jesus recognised that even among His believers, there are a lot of people who say things that they do not mean from their hearts, and He warned against this: **"Not every one that saith unto Me, Lord, Lord, shall enter into the Kingdom of Heaven; but they that doeth the will of My Father which is in Heaven"** (Matthew 7:21). People who encourage and accept flattery could find themselves walking on slippery grounds.

False praise may be given by parents because they want to make their children happy. Your friends may hide the truth from you for fear of hurting your feelings- a true friend should not! People may flatter their bosses in order to gain special favours from them, so watch out if you are a leader! Always find the courage to tell people the truth if you know it will help them, rather than giving them insincere praise that may eventually hurt them. The Bible says **"A flattering mouth worketh ruin."** (Proverbs 26:28)

Be open and humble when people give you negative feedback. Avoid favouritism by all means- it produces an atmosphere of insincerity and dishonesty. Discern when people are sweet-talking to win your favour and surround yourself with people who are not afraid to tell you the truth. When people know that we are open to loving and honest corrections and suggestions, rather than shallow flattery, they will be more inclined to tell us the truth even when it hurts.

For a moment the truth may hurt, but a lie hurts more in the long run. The American essayist and poet, Henry David Thoreau, said, "Rather than love, than money, than fame, give me the truth." Brave people want to hear the truth. Have the courage to receive the truth, and people will have the confidence to tell you things as they should be. Have the courage to tell the truth and people will respect you for it even if they do not love you.

Thirty Seven

DO NOT TRY TO PLEASE EVERYONE

"Care about what people think and you will be their prisoner." – Lao Tzu

"When a man's ways please the LORD, He maketh even his enemies to be at peace with him" (Proverbs 16:7). We are not in this world to please everyone. Too often we strive to please people at the expense of doing the right thing. People who are approval seeking may not stand up for what they believe, speak their mind or tell the truth at critical moments.

Here is a useful strategy to help overcome the need to please others: 1. Remember the times you said yes, when you really needed to say no, and the impact it had on you. 2. Never be in a hurry to say yes, especially if it is a major issue. Ask for more time to think through the request- this will save you from avoidable regrets. 3. Ask yourself, 'how will my saying yes impact on me and others in my cycle of influence?', and finally 4. Recognise that everybody will never be happy with you. No matter what you say or do, there will always be someone who doesn't like you or your decision.

The number one person you should seek to please at all times is God. ***"The fear of man bringeth a snare: but whoso putteth his trust in the LORD shall be safe"*** (Proverbs 28:25). Approval seekers can quickly fall prey to negative peer pressure- wanting to be like others in dressing, possessions and in living above their means. They may even forgo their rights and privileges so they can be liked by others. Trying to please everyone is simply putting yourself under unnecessary bondage.

People pleasers rarely protect personal boundaries- their time, convenience, and resources can be easily abused by others. People pleasing can kill creativity and freedom of expression, and confine an individual to a self-made prison. Whatever you do, you will be criticised anyway, so simply do what you know is right. Be free to be yourself and stop being defined and confined by the fear of what others think of you.

Trying to please everyone is a very hard job, and most of us will fail at it- because we are struggling to do the impossible. Many times when people seek others' approval, what they get is rejection and dejection. So, forget about pleasing people- start pleasing God and strive to live with a good conscience.

Thirty Eight

NURTURE YOUR IDEAS

***"Be less curious about people and more curious about ideas."* – Marie Curie**

Ideas are thoughts that generate in our minds intentionally or unintentionally. Ideas can be born when brainstorming, but they can also spark off when we are completely at rest, busy and at very odd times. Everything ever created originated from someone's idea.

Ideas are common to everyone; what makes the difference is what we do with them. Putting that thought down on paper helps you to focus on it and begin the process of making it a reality. The LORD said to the prophet Habakkuk, **"...*Write the vision, and make it plain upon tablets, that he may run that readeth it. For the vision is yet for an appointed time, but at the end it shall speak, and not lie: though it tarry, wait for it; because it will surely come, it will not tarry"*** (Habakkuk 2:2-3). God gives us gifts and creativity for the purpose of His kingdom and the blessing of humanity.

Failure in life is partly due to the fact that when God inspires us we either fail to take the first step, or we are too afraid to go all the way with His ideas. The Bible says, *"...the Lord...called by name Bezalel the son of Uri, son of Hur... and he has filled him with the Spirit of God, with skill, with intelligence, with knowledge..."* (Exodus 35:30-33). We are God's hands and feet; created as His workmanship to work in the lives of people on earth. Some people may be physically barren, but no one is ever completely barren of ideas.

Sometimes a good idea will stretch your faith to the point that you will need great courage to pursue it. Stop playing around with those thoughts. Write them down. Pray about them. Take the first step. Bring them to life.

If you do not act on your ideas, someone else will soon capture, nurture and make them a reality. Painfully, a lot of people have been shocked to find that what was once only an idea to them, has been showcased somewhere by another person. No one has the prerogative of any idea- they fly around, and whoever catches them first should either run with them or lose them. The life you seek today will be delivered to you by that simple or great idea in your mind.

Thirty Nine

GO AFTER YOUR GOALS

"Shoot for the moon. Even if you miss it you will land among the stars."- Les (Lester Louis) Brown

For how many years have you been trying to do things that will change your life without success? For a lot of people December to January every year is a period of frustration, self-condemnation and lamentation; yet a whole lot of people consider it a time to rise from the ashes, dust up themselves and start all over again.

Norman Vincent Peale stated, *"All successful people have a goal. No one can get anywhere unless he knows where he wants to go and what he wants to do or be."* All through this year keep your dreams in front of you. Refine and re-launch your goals. There is nothing wrong in starting all over when trip over; the danger is in giving up and completely losing hope. Therefore, *"... **take courage! Do not let your hands be weak, for your work shall be rewarded"*** (2 Chronicles 15:7).

Every year is 'pregnant' with miracles, signs and wonders. Everything you ever wanted to be is ever possible. Start where you are and stop worrying about where you should have been. Simply find a different way of doing things if you have had disappointing results in the past. Do not let the fear of failure prevent you from setting goals- the few things you desperately want to accomplish in the short, medium and long term.

Find 3-5 major things you would like to happen in the coming months. Break them into simple daily, weekly and monthly steps. Elbert Hubbard said, *"Many people fail in life, not for lack of ability or brains or even courage but simply because they have never organized their energies around a goal."* If you really thought of doing outstanding things in the coming months and years, without daily and weekly basic steps to get you there, you are simply day-dreaming.

Spend the next few days to **"Prepare your work outside; get everything ready for yourself..., and after that build your house"** in 2017. (Proverbs 24:24). *"A goal without a plan is just a wish."* (Antoine D. S Exupery) Remember, wishes rarely come true. When you set and pursue your goals you can turn the invisible into the visible. Your moderate goals will turn into moderate success, and your lofty goals can turn into awesome achievements.

Forty

FOCUS ON YOUR DESTINATION

"If you chase two rabbits, both will escape."

Former British Prime Minister, Winston Churchill, once remarked, *"You will never reach your destination if you stop and throw stones at every dog that barks."* What a true statement! Remember, as noted in yesterday's devotional, you are entering into a new year- a journey of another twelve months. There are a number of things you would like to accomplish before you complete the journey- may be one, two, three, four or even five. Your greatest obstacle will be lack of focus.

There will be problems, discouragement and distractions. It does not matter how big or little your goal may be, you need to concentrate all your energies to make it happen. The Bible suggests we should learn lessons on focus from the ant: *"It has no commander, no overseer or ruler, yet it stores its provisions in summer and gathers its food at harvest."* (Proverbs 6:7-8) You need a selective, narrow-minded and laser guided approach to clutching that trophy you yearn for. You cannot succeed at everything but you can be a master at something- and that can only happen through focus.

Focus on your goal day and night. Intentionally choose your friends, hobbies and learn to align with the dream that you have. Protect your time, emotions and health jealously so that they can support the fulfilment of your goals. Deliberately invest, network, study and save to enhance the new life you crave. The books you read, trainings you attend and the purchases you make should be geared towards your goals. This is the real focus- nothing less will do.

If you try to sit on two chairs at the same time you will find yourself in the middle; the middle in anything is never good enough. Simply make a list of what you have to do (or not do) as you enter into the New Year. Stick to the list and refuse to be distracted. ***"Let your eyes look directly forward, and your gaze be straight before you" (Proverbs 4:25).*** Take your mind off past failure- the only thing you should do is to learn from them. Keep focused on the destination you are going, not the distractions on your way, nor the success you have made. Dwelling on what went wrong or what could have been, will only dissipate your energy and derail you from the track of progress. Your life will drift towards the direction of your focus- whatever that is.

Forty One

DO NOT COMPARE YOURSELF WITH OTHERS

"But when they measure themselves by one another and compare themselves with one another, they are without understanding" (2 Corinthians 10:12).

Unhealthy self-comparison leads to insecurity. Too many people allow their moods and feelings to be dictated by how well they are performing compared to other people. Some people do this to the extent that they not only underrate themselves, but they go further to harbour feelings of jealousy, animosity towards others. How can we simply dislike someone just because they are ahead of us in certain areas; why would anyone allow someone else's progress to dictate their personal happiness and ability to relate with people? It would be more profitable to ignore, learn from, or altogether celebrate with others if they have excelled in certain areas.

We should rather work on ourselves and aim to be our best: ***"Do your best to present yourself to God as one approved, a worker who has no need to be ashamed..."*** (2 Timothy 13:5). When you feel upset that your colleagues are ahead of you, that is the result of negative comparison. There is nothing wrong in getting motivation from other people's achievements, or even aspiring to be greater than others.

Negative comparison can lead to self-inflicted hurts and pains such as unhappiness, depression, lack of confidence, the sin of resentment, and all sorts of negative attitudes towards others. The key thing to realise is that unhealthy comparison of ourselves with others does not change anything about us, except that we 'self-harm' by doing so. When you compare yourself with others, you diminish yourself compared to them. If you feel you are less than anyone else just because you do not have the same level of success, you are underrating the value that God places on you. Stop comparing yourself because your beginning might be someone else's middle, your middle might be some else's end and the start of your second quarter might be someone's third quarter.

Forty Two

LOOK AFTER YOUR MIND

"When negative thinking changes, everything changes."- Toni Sorenson

A positive mind-set is the foundation for a happy life. Former First Lady of the United States, Martha Washington, once said, "The greatest part of our happiness or misery depends on our dispositions and not on our circumstances. We carry the seed of the one or the other about with us in our minds wherever we go."

Negative and pessimistic thinking will produce a negative and defeated life. No matter how good and able a person is, if they continually accommodate hopeless thoughts, they are likely to end up with defeat and failure. **"...Be renewed in the spirit of your mind; and...put on the new man, which after God is created in righteousness and true holiness."** (Ephesians 4:23-24). If a person changes their mind about anything, things will change correspondingly. We are not the victims of our circumstances; we are the products of our mind-set.

People that harbour failure are more likely to end up as failure. People that accommodate bitterness will manifest vengeance and hatred; those who fill their lives with hope will reap the results of hope. Negative thinking is the greatest obstacle to success any one can contend with. The Bible, says ***"Finally, my brethren, whatsoever things are true, whatsoever things are honest, whatsoever things are just, whatsoever things are pure...if there be any virtue, and if there be any praise, think on these things."*** (Philippians 4:8) Begin and end the day with positive thoughts, no matter how bad things are. Negative thinking finds reasons why things cannot be done, positive thinking searches for reasons why things can be done. A negative state of mind can ultimately 'sink' a person's life.

All life's battles are fought and won in the mind. Losers lose first in the mind, and there are no stronger prisons than mental prisons. Former U.S. president, Ronald Reagan, states, "There are no constraints on the human mind, no walls around the human spirit, and no barriers to our progress except those we ourselves erect." Negatively minded people shut themselves against positive experiences and opportunities, because a person will mostly get what they expect. They are more likely to express negative emotions such as anxiety, fear, anger, frustration and irritability. The price of living with a negative state of mind is more expensive than anyone can afford.

Forty Three

LET GO OF UNHELPFUL TRADITIONS

"Just because something is tradition is no reason to do it, of course." Lemony Snicket

A tradition is a custom or belief passed on from generation to generation. These include ways of doing things, rituals and conventions. Traditions may be national, continental, religious, family, academic or those practiced by any group- a lot of them are in conflict with God's Word. The Bible says, **"Beware lest any man spoil you through philosophy and vain deceit, after the tradition of men, after the rudiments of the world, and not after Christ"** (Colossians 2:8). Traditions become problematic when they have their roots in Satan.

If the way of doing things where you come from stand between you and the Word of God, or negatively impact on how you relate with others, then something is wrong with it. A lot of spouses let their culture or tradition override the Word of God in their marriage (relationship). "We don't want tradition. We want to live in the present and the only history that is worth a thinker's dam is the history we make today."- Henry Ford.

Some cultures tend to minimise the importance of children or young people respecting their parents or older people, and many more perceive women as some kind of objects that should be used. Jesus warned against these attitudes: ***"He answered and said unto them, why do ye also transgress the commandment of God by your tradition?"*** (Matthew 15:3). There is nothing wrong with cultures and traditions so long as they do not interfere with your obedience to God's Word. We must ***"Have nothing to do with godless myths and old wives' tales; rather, train yourself to be godly"*** (1 Timothy 4:7). Even Church traditions should never be allowed to take precedence over God's Word in our lives.

It is great to sustain good traditions but those which blind-fold, limit and stand in the way of creativity and godly diversity should not be given any place in our lives. These can be enemies of progress, love and social interaction. Un-scrutinised tradition can lead to stagnation and mental imprisonment. Holding too dearly to certain traditions is the undoing of many people and society. Traditions are not always bad in themselves, but we should never allow ourselves to be enslaved by them.

Forty-Four

DEFEND YOURSELF CORRECTLY

"Assumptions are the termites of relationships." – Henry Winkler

Too often we react sharply to people's words, attitudes and actions directed at us because we thought (sincerely or not) that we were being attacked. Sometimes people air their opinion about us, and without thinking, we aim at them aggressively even though they have said nothing that warranted such reaction. People who react this way possibly do so because they have no trust in the other person or they feel vulnerable and uncomfortable around others.

We have heard several times that attack is the best form of defence, but in a lot of cases, what we actually need (especially in relationships) is not attack but a healthy defence. *"If possible, so far as it depends on you, live peaceably with all."* As much as you can, live peacefully with other people. This does not preclude disagreements and confrontations, rather it means we should never take things to the extreme when offended

(Romans 12:18). If you keep losing your cool, it could lead to aggression, isolation, and enmity. On the contrary, healthy defence leads to dialogue, damage control and peaceful co-existence. This applies whether you are at work, home or simply hanging out with others.

You can defend yourself without damaging relationships. You can be assertive without being aggressive. You can safeguard yourself without building a wall which could lead to self-isolation, frustration and self-imprisonment. One of the reasons why some young people carry knives is because they wrongly believe that someone is always out there to attack them. They tend to use the knives even when they are not under any threat.

Avoid anticipating confrontations; learn to sustain a positive conversation and find ways to defuse tension as you relate with people. It is alright to protect yourself from abuse, put downs and intimidations, but healthy defence is more productive than building fences. Tell yourself, 'no one is out to get me'. ***"... If God be for us, who can be against us?"*** (Romans 8:31).

We will always come across unreasonable and impossible people. We have a choice to either stay calm or let lose our negative emotions. It is always better to prevent things from escalating when faced with potentially volatile situations. Try not to always take things personally; learn to manage your emotions- this can be done through deliberate practice.

Forty-Five

PUT THE PAST BEHIND YOU

***"You do not move ahead by constantly looking in a rear view mirror."* - Dr Warren Wiersbe**

Ralph Waldo Emerson said: *"Finish each day and be done with it. You have done what you could; some blunders and absurdities have crept in; forget them as soon as you can. Tomorrow is a new day; you shall begin it serenely and with too high a spirit to be encumbered with your old nonsense."*

The past belong to history and lessons learned from history are very useful for the present. The past only has as much grip over us as we allow. Yesterday is past, don't mourn over it- it is irretrievable. Tomorrow is still in the making- look forward to it with excitement. Today is very important- make the most of it, it will soon be gone. John Newton remarked, *"We can easily manage if we only take, each day, the burden appointed to it. But the load will be too heavy for us if we carry yesterday's burden over again today, and then add the burden of the morrow before we are required to bear it."* Getting stuck in the past will drain your spiritual, physical and emotional energy.

God says: ***"Remember not the former things, nor consider the things of old. Behold, I am doing a new thing; now it shall spring forth, do you not perceive it? I will make a way in the wilderness and rivers in the desert."*** (Isaiah 48:18-19) Refuse to be limited by yesterday; look forward to tomorrow with hope. It is difficult to buy back the past; it is better to let go of the past. Make yesterday a rudder to guide you, not an anchor to ground you. As the clock ticks, days that are gone move faster behind you, and tomorrow accelerates towards you. Unless you plan for and focus on the future, it will soon become history and another cause for regrets.

Paul said: ***"Brethren, I count not myself to have apprehended: but this one thing I do, forgetting those things which are behind, and reaching forth unto those things which are before, I press toward the mark for the prize of the high calling of God in Christ Jesus."*** (Philippians 3:13-14) People who have experienced a glorious past can also become victims of their past. We are product of our past, but we shouldn't let the past hold us to ransom. Never stop trying no matter how bad things went the last time.

Forty Six

DEVELOP PASSION FOR ALL YOU DO

"Enthusiasm moves the world." – **Arthur Balfour**

"Passion is when you put more energy into something than is required to do it. It is more than just enthusiasm or excitement, passion is ambition that is materialised into action to put as much heart, mind, body and soul into something as is possible." – The Urban Dictionary

It takes passion to make a mark in life. Whether it is playing a musical instrument, earning a qualification, winning souls for Christ or having a successful marital relationship, passion is the key to excellence. It is not the only thing that counts in life, but without it other contributors to success may be rendered ineffective.

Jesus said, **"Blessed are those who hunger and thirst for righteousness, for they will be filled"** (Matthew 5:6). If we are not praying the way we should or do not see soul-winning as an urgent matter, we probably lack passion for the things of God. Jesus once told His followers, **"My food is to do the will of**

Him who sent me and to finish His work." (John 4:34) Passion is contagious; if we have it people will notice and catch it. It is like a hurricane that brings down anything that stands in its way. Lack of passion is the mother of all excuses.

Filled with passion, a salesperson with a fake, poor quality product will close more sales than the one with high quality product, and little passion. Without passion, it is possible to inherit great wealth and still end up a pauper; it is possible to be highly skilled and talented and still end up a failure. Passionate people demonstrate commitment, intensity and excitement in whatever they do. Passion is like wild fire, and no one can go far in life without it.

Henry for remarked, "You can do anything if you have enthusiasm...Enthusiasm is at the bottom of all progress. With it, there is accomplishment. Without it, there are only alibis." Enthusiasm conquers fear, wins over intelligence and skills and increases productivity. It is no respecter of age, it never bows to race and prejudice. Enthusiasm overcomes everything that comes across its way. It has the power to stir a crowd, start a revolution and change the world. The world needs one individual filled with passion far more than a thousand lukewarm people who lack fire within them. What is worth doing at all is worth doing with passion.

Forty Seven

KNOW YOUR WORTH

"What lies behind us and what lies before us are tiny matters compared to what lies within us." – Ralph Waldo Emerson

There once lived a man who was in love with old books. He overhead a friend talk about throwing away an old Bible that had been lying in the antic of his ancestral home for many years. The acquaintance remarked, "I was unable to read it", "Somebody called Guten-something had printed it." "You don't mean Gutenberg!" the old books enthusiast queried, in horror. "It was one of the first Bible ever printed, and a copy just sold for two million dollars!" His ignorant friend was unimpressed, and replied, "Mine wouldn't have sold for a dollar because someone called Martin Luther had made notes all over it in German."

Knowing our worth will determine how we comport ourselves and how we allow people to treat us. Too many believers have no clue how much value God places on them. They keep feeling worthless, irrelevant and de-motivated. They even settle for far less than God has ordained for them. They fail to understand that they are filled with, and surrounded by God's treasures. They continue to tolerate lack, poverty, shame and reproach. ***"... ye are bought with a price: therefore glorify God in your body, And in your spirit, which are God's."*** (1 Corinthians 6:20)

Many Christians compromise their faith and salvation for what the world has to offer, some even exchange their salvation for insignificant things. Ask God to open your eyes today to see beyond your current situation. No matter how negatively you perceive yourself, or how unfavourably others see you, God's opinion of you is what matters: ***"The LORD does not look at the things man looks at. Man looks at the outward appearance, but the LORD looks at the heart"*** (1 Samuel 16:7).

God places a high value on His people. He created, and made us partakers of His divine nature- your worth is determined by God. What you think you are worth is what the world will offer you. Satan and situations won't bow to you unless you show them what you are made of. The value you place on yourself will determine what you feed your body with. It will also dictate what you say and the kind of company you keep.

Forty Eight

WIN THE THREE DIMENSIONAL WARFARE

"A true Christian is one who has not only peace of conscience, but war within. He may be known by his warfare as well as by his peace."- J.C. Ryle

The Christian is constantly engaged in spiritual warfare. The devil and his agents are working twenty four hours every day to overcome God's children and hinder the work of the Kingdom. Paul prayed, *"And the very God of peace sanctify you wholly; and I pray God your whole spirit and soul and body be preserved blameless unto the coming of our Lord Jesus Christ."* (1 Thessalonians 5:28) The Bible differentiates between three compartments of man – Spirit, Soul, and Body. These three form the centre of spiritual warfare. To enjoy total victory over the enemy we have to defeat him in all three dimensions.

The human spirit is the part that knows God. The life of God is transmitted to your spirit at the New Birth. *"The spirit of man is the lamp of the Lord, searching all his innermost parts."* (Proverbs 20:27) *"The Holy Spirit bears witness with our spirit that we are the children of God."* (Romans 8:16) We need a healthy and strong spirit to be able to defeat the enemy at all times- so feed on God's Word, renew your spirit through worship and stay always connected to God through prayers.

Whereas the salvation of our spirit is instantaneous, the soul undergoes progressive change. The soul is the source of feelings, thoughts, desires, reasoning and personality- our emotions can give us away in spiritual warfare, our minds can defeat us ever before a battle begins. No matter how much a person prays and fasts, they will never enjoy total victory unless their mind accepts that God's Word guarantees their healing, prosperity and victory over the enemy.

The body or flesh is the outward, unchanged part of us with which we interact with the physical world through the physical senses. The Bible says in 1 Corinthians 9:27, **"But I keep under my body, and bring it unto subjection: lest that by any means, when I have preached to others, I myself should become a castaway."** The devil can attack the believer's body with sickness, weakness, disease, pain and other physical afflictions. The devil can also use fleshly indulgences to conquer a child of God. Until we win in all our three dimensions, we will only enjoy limited success in spiritual warfare.

Forty Nine

KEEP YOURSELF HUMBLE

"A great man is always willing to be little." – **Ralph Waldo Emerson**

"Humility is perfect quietness of heart. It is for me to have no trouble; never to be fretted or vexed or irritated or sore or disappointed. It is to expect nothing, to wonder at nothing that is done to me, to feel nothing done against me. It is to be at rest when nobody praises me and when I am blamed or despised."- Andrew Murray

God's Word says, **"... everyone who exalts himself will be humbled and he who humbles himself will be exalted"** (Luke 14:11). Many great people have fallen because of pride (Luke 14:11; James 4:10). Jesus is the perfect example of humility. He ate with, mingled with and dressed like the disciples and ordinary people. He washed the feet of His disciples and served them, leaving us an example to follow: **"Whosoever will be chief among you, let him be your servant: Even as the son of man came not to be ministered unto, but to minister"** (Matthew 20:27-28).

Humility is not wearing a cloak of inferiority; it is the recognition that whatever you are or have, originated from only one source- God. He has promised to ***'revive the spirit of the humble, and to revive the heart of the contrite ones.'*** (Isaiah 57:15)Humble people never talk too highly of themselves because they recognise that the source of every blessing is God. Humble people give and share credit. Humility is the only way to please God and get Him to pour His grace upon us.

Pride reduced angels to demons. Arrogance will bring down anyone, no matter how long it takes. If God blessed you with riches and resources, stay humble and He will never let you down. We can be great without looking down on others, strong and still be humble, rich and yet relate with the poor. This is true humility. *"Humility does not mean thinking less of yourself than of other people, nor does it mean having a low opinion of your own gifts. It means freedom from thinking about yourself one way or the other at all."*- William Temple.

Arrogance is an expression of weakness, kindness is a demonstration of strength; arrogance sheds the light on a person's level of insecurity, but respect for others shows that you are a person of great substance. Contempt for others is vanity and will eventually lead to a person's fall from grace.

Fifty

CONFRONT ISSUES,

DON'T COMPLAIN ABOUT THEM

A man was in a monastery and had a chance to speak only two words every five years. When asked to speak his first two words after five years, he said, "Food bad." When given the chance to speak another two words five years later he said, "Bed hard." The next five years when given another chance, his two words were, "I quit." The leaders of the monastery responded, "No surprise. All you have been doing since you came here is complain."

We can always find something to complain about. There is a difference between complaining and sincerely making suggestions, righteously fighting a good cause and genuinely working to make things right. I am not suggesting we should pretend when things are out of course, but the Bible says, ***"Do all things without murmurings and disputings."*** (Philippians 2:14) Finding fault overly never changes any situation, seeking a solution does. If we constantly criticise, condemn and complain, we make ourselves part of the problem. And when it comes to personal problems, you may complain to anyone who cares to hear you, but that does not mean they truly care. Some people will actually be pleased you have to go through those struggles.

People who always complain rarely accomplish anything. They usually contribute little or nothing to a problem situation. Complaining can be threat to your health, happiness and ability to solve problems. Choose to be a dreamer, a listener, a believer and a change agent.

Referring to the children of Israel in the wilderness, the Bible says, **"And don't grumble as some of them did, and they were destroyed by the angel of death."** (1 Corinthians 10:10) Complainers in God's house fail to realise that their fault-finding and defiance is not against the Church or God's people, but against God. Suggestions should always be welcome; positive criticism helps any person or group to improve but a bitter, critical and angry person will compound an already existing problem.

Moaners in the Church often have problems with their spiritual lives- stubborn hearts, lukewarmness and progressive backsliding. It is always better to find the positives in every situation and seek better ways to express our mind so we do not become obstacles to the work of God.

"If you don't like something, change it. If you can't change it, change your attitude. Don't complain." – Maya Angelaou

Fifty-One

OVERCOME INSECURITY

"Some trust in chariots, and some in horses: but we will remember the name of the LORD our God." **(Psalm 20:7)**

Security is a state of being free from danger or threat. Insecure people fear overly for their future and worry over and again about what life holds for them. Insecurity can manifest in the form of low self-esteem and feelings of incompetence and failure. Insecure people may feel unappreciated, unloved, and unwanted. Yes there may be genuine reasons to feel this way, but your feelings do not really matter when God is on your side. It is sometimes alright to feel insecure, so long as it drives us into the hands of God, and help us find ways to move forward in life.

You may not have much wealth; others may have gone well ahead of you; you may not like the way things are going generally in your life. If everything seems to be falling apart, *"... look not at the things which are seen, but at the things which are not seen: for the things which are seen are temporal; but the things which*

are not seen are eternal." (2 Corinthians 4:18). Insecurity can lead to error of judgement, failure to make progress and finger pointing at others. Build your hope only on God's love, and His ability and willingness to see you through.

Insecurity is the enemy's weapon to make people timid, hesitant and discouraged. It can affect every area of life- job, health and relationships. Many things can stand in people's way, but the most powerful of them lie within us. ***"They that trust in the Lord shall be as Mount Zion, which cannot be removed, but abideth for ever."*** (Psalm 125:1). Give your insecurities to God, and leave them with Him.

Refuse to dwell on what people say or think about you, what God thinks about you matters more than anything else. Confident people do not tear others down. Happy people tend to make others happy too.

Self-comparison is a product of insecurity. Stop wishing you were someone else. Your looks, personality, nationality and whatever it is about you that you don't like, are there for a reason. Be secure in yourself, and you will be happy the rest of your life.

Fifty-Two

SPREAD YOUR WINGS

"Have not I commanded thee? Be strong and of a good courage; be not afraid, neither be dismayed: for the LORD thy God is with thee whithersoever thou goest" (Joshua 1:9).

"It is not the critic who counts, not the man who points out how the strong man stumbled or where the doer of deeds could have done better. The credit belongs to the man who is actually in the arena; whose face is marred by dust and sweat and blood; who strives valiantly; who errs and comes short again and again...; who, at the best, knows in the end the triumph of high achievement; and who, at the worst, if he fails, at least fails while daring greatly, so that his place shall never be with those cold and timid souls who know neither victory nor defeat."- Theodore Roosevelt.

We all regret the chances we failed to take, the times we failed to flap our wings and the change we hesitated to make. If we wait until we are ready or no longer afraid, we will never achieve much. **"For God has not given us a spirit of fear, but of power and of love and of a sound mind"** (2 Timothy 1:7). Max DePree notes, *"We cannot become what we want to be by remaining where we are"* Until we are ready to die trying, we will never truly live.

God will not abandon you when you act in faith. The better life we long for is located in the territories we are too scared to go. *"Don't fear failure so much that you refuse to try new things. The saddest summary of life contains three descriptions: could have, might have, and should have."* (Louise E. Boone). God has set before you an open door. Why should you be held back by too much caution? If it looks stupid, risky, scary and too much to attempt- it is probably the right thing to do. Give it a go.

You will make mistakes, things will not be perfect- they will never be. Having the skill to do something is important. Having the desire to do it is as important. But having the commitment to do it is what brings success. We learn to walk, not by taking instructions, seeking encouragement or by watching others take steps. We learn to walk by getting up, taking the first step, falling over, getting up and doing it again.

CONCLUSION

I hope you have enjoyed reading this book? God moves in our lives in several ways. Also, there are several things in life that come together to make us the kind person God wants us to be. These fifty-two golden nuggets were written so that God can use them to add something to your life as you prayerfully read through them and ask God for grace to apply what you have read. They are carefully written with you in mind and I pray as you put the book down for this period, you will find it so useful that you will flip through the pages from time to time and find some help and inspiration for future use.

We are able to do a lot more in life when we step out of our comfort zone, take a risk and pursue our dream. Winners do not let current issues of life stop them, rather they learn from problems, continue to make progress, and never rest until the desires of their heart come to pass. Instead of surrendering to fear, they surrender their fears to God and depend on His power to take them through the challenges they face. This is what victory is about and I trust that the short chapters of this book have inspired you into pursuing your dream and not let the enemy stand in your way. Stay blessed.